Falling off the Twig

J. D. Stewart

ISBN - 13:978-1503317178
ISBN - 10:150331717X

Table of Contents

Introduction

The British have an expression, falling off the twig. It means to die. It would seem from this phrase that the falling is due to something that was done wrong, some sort of slip up that caused the falling. The problem is that, if we do everything right and hold to life, we will still fall off the twig. It is a ponderable that is guaranteed to occur with time.

In a real, not a metaphorical sense, leaves fall. It is an event that is repeated in deciduous trees every Fall. As a cycle there is usually no death, just a yearly dormancy in which the tree leaves fall off. Plants suggest through their winter dormancy, which is observed seasonally, what people experience not seasonally but death for all time. When we observe the similarities we are more often struck by the differences. Both people and plants die, but people seem to be considered disparately as either returning of the body to the soil and never more to be seen, reduced it ash or resurrected through belief in an afterlife to a higher form. These considerations are awe inspiring, two understood empirically, while the last consideration is usually based on some understanding of faith. However, we seem to take the death in humans as an impersonal event in an impersonal world in which we are excluded from death's reality. We do not seriously consider our own death nor do we see it as necessarily as a form of dormancy from which we will return to living.

Yet, another scenario, the most amazing aspect of any may not be the mechanics of any possibility following death. The most interesting and baffling consideration may be that most people give no thought to death or hide its ultimate impact in euphemistic phrasing like falling from the twig, kicking the bucket or joining the choir eternal. Why do we not consider the finality and the loss of everything that we have learned and all that we know? Years of practiced living may be worthy of less serious and concentrated thought, despite the fact that ultimately for each person death will occur as a certainty while defining the most significant event in our lives.

From the earliest time we are guarded from disease by parents who take us to the doctor, prepare for our learning by putting us in the right schools and hope that we will find the right mate for a good life and for fecundity to continue the lineage. At every turn our next moves are anticipated and plans are generated for the immediate and long, distant future. We plan for our retirement by saving and sometimes develop elaborate scenarios like where we will spend our remaining days which may be imagined to be far from our work lives, living our lives as we have never before doing different things in different places — a new world without a thought of the days of toil and possibly the long hours of stress and pressure to sell or produce.

What makes us avoid the ultimate question about the final reality in our earthly lives? A friend just told me that his father who is now dead but lived into his eighties would walk away from conversations about death. He did not want to think about death. Two friends told my wife about a wreck on the interstate in which their car was burned as was at least one of the occupants of one of the other five vehicles involved. All tolled, three people died in the accident. My friends were not scratched or bruised but walked away from the tragedy scarred by the event when, as far as their cost, they only had to replace glasses, clothes and prescriptions. Although I consider these two friends to have a good handle on their death, this was too close to not give them a start. They pondered the loss of those lives and the fact that they were spared. This was very traumatic for my dear friends and reflects the sobering and stoic reality of approaching death so traumatically.

This book tries to sort out the issues surrounding death, those sobering concerns that drive us to avoid, and less often embrace, the last event of each of our lives. Some find no reason to even consider that there might be something, life or etherial existence after one passes from the earth. The fact that many do not entertain the possibility of an afterlife but go into that dark night without hope only to assume that they will eventually be returned to the soil, to the elemental forms from which they arose, makes the subject of this book very important, if not ultimately important.

Chapter 1

Life as a Series of Reactions

In Albert Camus's book, *The Plague*, we are given the images and understandings of a gated city in the throes of pestilence. Some ignored the death-dealing roll of the dice, others feared it and some did the best they could to avoid the thoughts that accompany being quarantined with those that were infected and dying in agony and with the dead that were decaying in the streets. In some cases people became more social, doing those things that social animals do when all is right, but to excess. Although excessive behaviors may seem peculiar and overly dramatic this inappropriate reaction to death or its intimations may actually represent the way that many react to the threat of mortality. We may stand in denial against death and separation and behave as if everything is fine: enjoying each day as if it were to go on forever.

We are active and reactive people. Moderns always think that something can always be done to improve ours or other's lives. Science technology and medicine have given us the distinct belief that we can be pulled back from the edge of peril due to any threatening condition. This Baconian optimism, however, is less than a belief for those that seemingly have no hard and fast expectations for death, who seem to acquiesce only to life possibly under the shadow of misfortune or opprobrium. But we all string the wishes and hopes of our lives into a plan to provide the most opportunities to do and to look forward, with some going so far as to strangle convention for the breathe of unacceptable liberality. We string together those things, often in rapid succession, which we must do and the things that we wish to do from which we derive great pleasure without any thought of outcome.

Regardless of our intent to good or bad, the things that we must do are generally penciled in first, followed by the things we believe we have earned the right to enjoy because we have not failed in doing the necessities. We often dread the necessities and hold on to the time spent doing the pleasurable things. We are sequential utilitarians who try to spend as little time in the sequence of events tied to the painful requisites and allotting the maximum amount of time for the pleasurable. This pleasurable progression may become extended to days and weeks or more as pleasure clouds our thoughts and helps to guard against the realities of necessary behavior, and those concerned with our ultimate terminus.

It may be that amid the succession of occurrences we allow no interference since interfering with the scheduling of necessities may reduce the pleasurable events in number or time spent and may cause a cascading of irresponsibility with time wasting events truncating a well planned future. Each person attempts to reset the order as best one can. But no matter the effective sequencing or the extent of pleasurable and painful activities the elements of life that produce temporal happiness are the focus of our lives. We never end the expanse of time we have spent planning to insure maximum enjoyment perhaps until death surprises us and we face a potentially fatal illness. Our push to enjoy our time without such grave consideration may force all meaningful consideration about our possible demise from our minds.

I remember when a tool that I had ordered came in the mail. It was claimed that it could easily remove paint from woodwork, but the ease of use was no consolation. I was livid. It arrived the day before I was to start a two week vacation at home. I had caught up with my work to insure that the time away from the lab would be optimized for what I had planned; this tool was now to cut into my pleasure and destroyed my plan. I was fuming. All during the paint-removing experience, I was mad at everybody and everything. Since all the plans that I had made for my time off were irrevocably lost. I guess I was mad at myself but projected my anger onto everything and everyone else. The delivery interfered with my pleasurable vacation time, it was a responsibility I wanted to avoid as it crept into my time of pleasure, which I felt should have been off-limits to employer or at home work.

Yet no matter the amount or duration of pleasurable events in life's schedule, we have limits in our vision of pre-planned time. It may be a vacation, a time at the beach, a trip to Europe, any of which may become locked in our memories against responsibilities to be retrieved when we are feeling trapped by necessity and drudgery, but any pleasurable distraction that may takes us away from the common toil may end for a time with the death of a loved one that interrupts our plans. We then do all that is necessary to carry us over the time of this emergency attempting, where possible, to get back to the necessary sequencing to maximize the pleasurable while meeting the responsibilities that must be fulfilled. But pleasurable diversion will not appropriately subdue any thought of another's death when they are close to us. Yet we want to forget about death. We steel ourselves believing that we are destined to thrive, survive and maximize our pleasure while the reality of death is seen as a concern of others, and we do have to get over our grief and return to our daily responsibilities. We try hard to get over our grief and replace it with daily activities.

We can never get our minds around the possibility that our plans could be interrupted. There is not a plan B. All our plans cannot fail. Although plans being changed due to death are infinitely more serious than my vacation time being eaten up by work on my house, it is impossible to believe that our pleasure is going to be interfered with by the unexpected and ultimate reality of death in our families.

At the same time the parents are planning the life of their child from an early age, the father and mother are launching a plan for their retirement and old age. Everything from emergency money to paying the cat's vet bill may be adequately considered. The funeral plot and the casket, the ceremony and the headstone may be contracted for and the gravestone put in place with names and birth dates. The only dates missing are those for the final inscription, the death date.

Everything that we plan is for events prior to our death, but the topic of death may never arise in family conversation even if a will is drawn up or a stone for the grave is purchased. Death like every other unplanned event in life is a reaction, an unavoidable reaction to our state of health or the response to an unexpected and unplanned event or series of events bring life to an end. How should we respond to death as an unexpected yet definite end to a sequence of events that interrupts a primarily pleasurable life? We seem to believe in some way that the grave plot, the stone or the will will not need to be seriously considered for an indeterminately long time. Death only in the abstract seems to touch our consciousness.

Chapter 2

Cultural Importance in Death

Some cultures incorporate death into their daily lives through ancestry worship while some may actually bring the dead into their dwelling places and pray and consult with them as those who have made the full transition to wisdom and the other side successfully. It may be that the dead are petitioned for wisdom since they may have since death gained full wisdom or that they have traveled the full breadth of life. It has been the case that some primitive tribes have eaten the vanquished in order to gain the strength of those that were overcome in battle. This practice was thought to empower the conquers with the physical strength of those conquered thus augmenting battle prowess. The dependency on the dead in Western cultures is not uniformly experienced other than an occasional trip to the gravesite for a few words from a dependent grieving child or adult.

Death was considered a crowning glory for the rulers of ancient Egypt. The embalming of the Egyptian pharaohs, the preservation of Vladimir Lenin in Moscow and of Jeremy Bentham represents in some sense the inability of the living to let go of their leaders and thinkers. Bentham who was on display at London College as a chimera of wax, bones and hair, appears to have avoided complete decay. Bentham was finally secured in storage after attempts by miscreants to repeatedly vandalize his remains possibly a mockery of death. Lenin's remains have been on display in Moscow since his death in the early 1920s and have been viewed by the public, except during the second World War. Eva Peron was not buried for over twenty years after her death. Her embalmed remains were on view and it was said that she was idolized by Argentinians, her affectionate public who no less adored her in death.

But all of these mummified remains were not seen so much as personally known loved ones but rather as symbols of leadership, thought, kindness or beauty. The idea of honoring the dead seems strange when the topic of death, in our culture, is usually not discussed in detail before the fact. Extreme disabilities may cause friends to discuss an invalid's downward momentum in muffled tones. Few plans are discussed among loved ones and certainly not with the one who is ill and possibly dying.

Since America is now a youth culture, it would seem strange to revere the dead after trying to avoid recognition of the pre-dead as they were in their decline or even their productive years. To be honored by the young is for one to be a rock star, vital and ever animated, blessed with the blush of youth and a general lack of concern for anything that transcends the immediate. Even the intellectual interests in gender, race and multiculturalism is either a chance or planned avoidance of specific true heroes of our culture while alternatively exalting those who have contributed to cultural study. The hero is a thing of the past for most young people. Having lead lives — at least many have — in which a father, mother or siblings have done very

16

little to contribute to the modeling of heroic behavior with the concept being lost with the past, students at a high school recently eschewed the history of our nation wanting today's history, wanting no direction nor influential guidance from past failures and successes. Thus you are not exposed to those cause-effect scenarios that would drop a pall on dogmas. A full accounting of history is sacrificed or at least rewritten or truncated and directed toward the study of specific areas of faddish cultural interest or predispositions. The now has been given over to attractive pundits, the new heroes and history makers, who without having to change the world must only look good in it and communicate the right guarded perspectives on life.

In addition to the new historicity that tends to avoid the brave of the dead from the past, Americans seem to evade discussions of the realities of their own deaths yet may selectively rejoice and immerse themselves instead in their trip to France, perhaps, or some other positive remembrance or planned trip as a deflection to avoid the consideration of the inevitability of their deaths. Even those that are great, or greatly honored, when preparing their memoirs may dwell on the past looking for greatness to be found among their living actions, while few to none seriously consider that when they die. There may be even dubious speculation concerning ones post-earthly prospects. John Dewey, our most noted American philosopher, did not look to heroism. He felt that those that are so honored must be only selected for recognition after death, but since everyone must have autonomous authority in granting heroic status to the dead, the life may not be honored and no heroes proclaimed.

17

Heroism is a personal decision that does not rate veneration. This individualized view of heroics or not prevents a consolidated recognition in revered behavior. In this regard, even in death greatness may not be favored, and if not then anyone could have the same heroic statue as any one else. If we "lose" someone it would be hard to say that he or she was special, especially heroic.

Famous last words can be a continuation of the striving for earthly recognition. As a notable grammarian said last, " I am about to or I am going to die; either expression is correct." A horticulturalist had scratch into the alabaster a short verse. "Here I lie in my eternal home, a rich supply of fertile loam. " Both have at the end of their lives denied the seriousness and finality of death by being rather clever, but neither gives any concern to the obviation of seriousness and finality for which death calls each of us.

It is not a concern for the living and breathing after or during the event but during the many years of life for which close consideration may produce correction or at least amelioration of hostility and evil. In recent decades the final viewing of the body, the proof of death's finality, is often by passed for a memorial service in which the dead are frequently laid to rest in near deification despite any possible glaring offenses at least half remembered from their lives. Honoring one does not guarantee that the evil that they might have produced will be honestly and rightly censored but more probably eulogized for the hearers. I have a pastor friend who refuses to deliver the funeral message for one who is obviously not worthy of such venerable last words. Even the term "passing" instead of death, buried and gone, does seem to gloss over the ineluctable reality of deaths cold hand. Most funeral services are a less than honest adumbration of a former life. We use the term that was once an ethnic reference to the dying process - passing. The person in reality has not passed from life to death in the common understanding but has rather ceased to be and resides in some vague, assumed etherial locus without definition, name or defined agreeability. While the truth is that the dead will never be engaged in conversation or proclaim love to another they are surely gone and vagary cannot hide the loss. We die and the pain and heartache that may plague the living for our death has serious and longterm consequences for those left on earth, if, with time, the loved one is remembered at all. A friend was burned and his ashes were place in an area behind a bar in which he occasionally worked for his relatives did not want him, but they took all of his possessions including an apartment complex. He was left for paying customers and fellow workers to gawk at his picture taped to a black cardboard box full of ashes.

In contrast to the cultures that may embalm loved ones that have died and keep them in their dwellings, we, by law, are to bury our loved ones in a death grouping, a cemetery, which is usually found by law today, at the outskirts of the community or city, where accidentally seeing and thus being reminded of the sad even tragic event is reduced: the dead are only to be visited on anniversaries or birthdays, dressed with flowers and forgotten for another year. Some may be turned to ashes and spread on the earth or ocean, leaving no permanent trace. Those that keep the ashes

19

even on a mantel or coffee table, may strain to find the person present in their daily life, but this is a stretch honoring the dead when body parts with bone are reduced to the sweepings of a fireplace. This ashy residue creates little understanding of an eternal life as a bowl of minerals which would require more expense and effort to reconstitute for some useful purpose by the living than is realistically practical. At best the ashes are suitable for changing the color of a hydrangea or for dusting the daffodils.

Ours is a youth culture as the decaying skin of older life is tugged, stretched and sewn to effect younger appearance in life as their preservation in death is likewise accomplished by most bodies put on display for last visitation. Joan Rivers died at 81 and was virtually unrecognizable from her plastic-surgical "improvement."An elderly relative of my wife died, the comment was made that that old lady, at one hundred years of life and imbalmed, looked better than most of the mourners in attendance at the funeral. A youthful look or the surgical practice of youth-making may give the illusion of youth and health, but does not turn back the hands of time and forestall death.

Our steps merely stumble at the death of an acquaintance or loved one. We then hurry back to our pursuit of the living: living everyday and not fixing on the lessons that death in life has to teach. A bridge by which people chose their last fatal act on earth was considered the villain for those that jumped from it to their deaths. We tweak the occurrence of death in such a way as to offer a respite as a suicide barrier was to be erected to prevent jumpers from the bridge, to prevent people from taking their own lives. A father who lost a son commented that the bridge which had been named by some the Bridge of Death, was to no longer take the lives of loved ones. How sad for those left behind, how self-deceiving to imagine that someone who wished to take their lives could not find another way. Most of the lost are lost because their was never a productive method for quelling these desires to end their lives. Perhaps a seldom realistically faced reality of death created an image that was appealing to those that were suicidal rather than causing those considering suicide to realize that if death was not the end then more thought should be given to taking one's own life since this consideration could have great importance in viewing any possible post-earthly destination.

Chapter 3

Religious Beliefs and Death

There are beliefs that make this connection between life and death more important. Religious tenets often promise life after death. When ideology or laziness cause us to suspend reason by a failure to deal with death, we focus on other less important issues in our lives and fail to cobble beliefs in establishing a complete understanding of life and death as a holistic event. Other cultures, as mentioned earlier, have integrated a consideration of death and its aftermath into their lives. The Hindus who believe that an expectation for life and behavior during this life will determine the type of incarnation in the next. Despite the importance of behavior in this life in that culture there is an incongruous failure to care for others who are subject to eking out a life of poverty in the gutters. There is no help for these lowly cast members by those more fortunate and their qualified goodness and considerably better lives. For to interfere with one's caste fate is to jeopardize the incarnation of all concerned by a potentially humbling next life which may result in indwelling some lesser animal possibly over and over again until ultimately the cycling of souls ends. Why would this encourage anyone to adopt such a faith? Where some worship their ancestors, these faithful are best to not step on ants or eat those animals in the cycle states of cows.

While some Asians may think that they will be punished for inappropriate or wrong behavior in life, they must give thought to their actions in the constraints of karma and dharma and the punishment of interfering with the fate of another person. Those that believe in human reincarnation have little reason to concern themselves with any thoughts of death. To be returned to human life is a net gain of zero except the possibility that the indwelling will not be as pleasant or affluent as previous incarnations and one is armed only with the outside possibility of enduring wisdom gleaned from previous existence. Yet how this might benefit an ant or a fly incarnation is difficult to imagine.

The person that finds no reason to believe that their is any reasonable argument for life after death, and that we are soulless and in time will return to the elemental aspects of nature, has good reason to consider his or her life before it ends. Everything that can be accomplished depends on the time given to complete one's tasks. On the other hand, if there is no accounting for the way one uses one's life, why would you do anything that does not focus on you and provide you, by any means possible, with the things that you want in a feverish drive to get anything you want by any means possible? Murder, robbery, rape may get you what you want, and without retribution from wronged individuals and the law; you can have it all. There is nothing that an atheist can hold up as a foundation for civil life except fear of being caught getting everything that you want by any way you can. Unfortunately for the atheist, the protections that we all enjoy among one another are based on the belief that their is a time of punishment for wrong doing and if not in this life then the next. This belief and the foundational belief that the governance of this world is tied to a God who controls all time and judgment — a God of final and ultimate judgment, then there will be an accounting for our actions, not always in this life, but in the next life in which we are not to be given the form of an animal but as ourselves standing possibly in the defendant's box.

The consideration that should be given by everyone that justice may not allow any of us to escape our punishment for what we may have done in life, is one that cannot be set aside without a callous disregard for self and for others. If on the other hand you consider that judgment may be an overreach but realize that, if you are wrong in your expectations, then you will be facing an experience for which you have not prepared you mind and guided your life. You may have made ultimately the worst choice or your life. Alternatively the prospects of suffering, from the shear arrogance of any shortsighted assumption, by being cast into the body of an ant, a cow or a slug or find yourself in an endless cycle of human existence in dwellings in which you may not be able, due to circumstance, to effectively carry over wisdom or knowledge from your previous incarnations, are less than encouraging.

This gamble over expectations has eternal consequences. In most religions evil living in this life is punished in the next. You will not, if indeed you do return to life, any form of life, if you return to what you know or even have the ability to know and learn from your trials and tribulations before your death, you may be able to control this reanimation of yourself. To consider having a life before death, in which one has limited means to produce the life one would want, is just as unlikely as determining the life you will have in wishing after death. To consider that you will continue to inhabit new bodies of people or animals is an extremely dangerous bet, when one would expect most of us if not all should have some memory of past lives, yet few even claim to recall such incarnations. It would seem that most that do claim such reincarnations are usually not followers of the Indian sects where there maybe more knowledge of such past lives, but appear to be those who have merely taken the idea without much of the religious trappings as a reasonable expectation at death.

The bet, according to Blaise Pascal, given in his *Pensées*, is that you should make a "wager" that what you believe has a large probability to be realized — after all he was a mathematician. But whatever you decide, you will ultimately reap the result of your wager. The light thinker may imagine that you will go where ever you believe you will go, and that what ever your idea of the afterlife will be yours simply because you believe it. The atheist, will hold to finding unconscious nothingness, or should I say; he or she will not realize the dark night resulting from the life chosen to live . If you believe in reincarnation or you are a pantheist or panentheist your understanding of what you had counted on may not be inviting, a return to the elemental form, or even a knowable after life for all the hard lessons which life has dealt you.

Pascal also encourages us to consider that decisions made in our finite lives should be considered as possibly having eternal consequences. Decisions in life are wagers and should not be thought only as worldly decisions but may have the overriding impetus of other-worldly effects. The best bet, on which to hinge your after death experience, is to consider the wager and make it on the basis of the loss of the finite life, which is a certainty, for the uncertain but infinite possibility of a new and better or worse life after death. Pascal thought that this was a good wager and added that if it were to prove untrue you have lost nothing, but, if it is to be proven true, then you may inherit eternal life, a wonderful life, because you embraced the belief in the Christian God through faith in Jesus Christ.

Belief is not arbitrary in the argument about wagers. Pascal bases his argument on the free belief in Jesus as the propitiation and salvation of your soul which shall live forever with God in a perfected body, without pain and disease. His message is that if you place your faith in the Christian God and his son Jesus that you would rule with Jesus as his brother or sister in a glorious existence forever. What does forever mean? To define forever or eternity is to imagine a small bird picking up a grain of sand every thousand years and when all the sands of the earth are removed by this small bird, eternity would have just begun. This imperfect analogy given many times over the years would indicate that a limitless amount of time in heaven with Jesus, say, is better than an unfounded wager that you will simply exist in some form or return to the earth, at least as far as Pascal can see.

Pascal's wager requires the existence of eternity. Why should we believe in eternity? We can believe in time which seems to play games with out lives. Time seems arbitrary in that when we need more time, time seems to fly, and when we have time on our hands, it seems to slow down. Time seems relentless in its arbitrary rule over our lives. It does not quit when we die, or at least when we have experienced the death of others. Why should it stop for us? If we continue to inhabit this planet or living entities in all varieties, if we continue to live on seemingly indefinitely, can we not imagine a long, very long time, an eternity, time without end. Why should this time frame be only for the living, in fact, why should not all places in the universe have the same time and forever? Einstein showed that time could vary under certain circumstances. We may be the captives of both our time and the time that "lives" on beyond us. Our history, whether written or not, will be confined to our time in life. Why should time not also maintain control over us in our deaths. Why can we be sure that time, even eternity, will not follow us after death. In the overall of things, time is the constant and we are the variables. If we stay in time we must succumb to its rules. To ride the time line day following day, year following year without end, we must exist as appropriate travelers dressed for a new place, a new time and hopeful that all that has past will have meaning on our new journey.

The stakes are high. The wager is free, but you risk getting the reward of heaven and eternal life by betting your life which you ultimately do not have to gamble. For you will lose your wager with time, if you make no decision at all. The wager costs only what you cannot hold on to, life. As the saying goes, you may get what you cannot buy for what you cannot hold on to, life. This wager makes guessing at all other possibilities for death seem insanely inferior. To risk a few years for an eternity of existence in paradise, is foolish, and if you guess wrong, eternity will last forever and you in it for all time and very possibly not to your liking.

Chapter 4

Life and Death Continuum

After an accident or during a surgery and before being brought back to consciousness some have said that they saw a white light or thought they were seeing the "other side." This has caused some to finally give some thought to death. Most come to the conclusion that what ever they saw was the most life changing event of their lives. It is difficult to say what these people experienced when their brains were possibly deprived of oxygen or numbed by anesthetic. It is a good argument regardless that it probably does not fill in the spaces between what we know and experience on earth and what by accident or surgical anesthesia we may imagine has been a glimpse into our future. Most, however, are obsessed with their experience upon being revived. For these people the question should be raised, what are we doing or not doing that seems to be influenced by this interstitial event of death or near death before one's time.

Atheists say that they are good people and that is all that is legally required of any citizen and beyond life is the ineluctable reality of bodily decay and that there is no judgment because there is no Judge. And those that believe in an afterlife after seeing the white light or the other side still have to determine what will allow them to permanently enjoy what they think they glanced in the afterlife. Will measurable improvement in behavior be needed? What could possibly be required for a generic understanding of life or death? If this doubt is not raised then the obsession with death should bring the same consideration of life's meaning and what awaits beyond the bright light. The consideration that death is little more than one's molecules and atoms being returned to the earth seems a bit simplistic with the possibility of eternal dispositions beyond the soil and one's ability to control one's future even in death, while pondering that we have not done enough in case their is a final rendering of souls from bodies which, if rightly considered, must strike a stark tone of ill-preparedness with grave consequences.

Provocative, although of dubious scientific value, was the weighing of six humans and fifteen dogs on each of their death beds and finding that four of the six human lost an average of 15 grams of weight, while in contrast no loss of weight was noted in the case of the dogs at death. Dr. MacDougall's experiment in 1901 was attacked and he was ridiculed for his work. Technical and interpretive errors have left this experiment behind without scientific merit. But the possibility of their being a soul released from the body at death is still as provocative as this failed early twentieth century experiment failed to show. For the possibility of a soul inhering in the human corporeal being, which is lost at death but continues its existence outside of the body still holds powerful meaning for many cultures. The soul must not be confused with the spirit, that vital force of all humans and not dogs and other animals. The soul appears to be the inherent identifier which would seem a mooring for our heart, head and spirit and a person-identifiable intermediary for the spirit. Both soul and spirit appear to be lost from the body at death and hold the animating and identifying character of the live entity.

Was their something to lose when cremation yields only the elemental forms of the remains? Is there something else that this poorly designed experiment could suggest besides the fact that the doctor had expectations for his results much as modern scientists sculpt or massage experimental answers to fulfill support for a preordained hypothesis. If there is anything to this questionable work, it again raises the danger of inculcating prejudice into experimental results that would without close evaluation be seen as proof of the transcendence of the soul, but more germane to the argument here is the failure to consider death before it occurs both for the ultimate disposition of the soul.

Perhaps religious beliefs assume an afterlife, but what is the impetus for such assumptions throughout recorded history and across the earth? From where does this strong belief, no matter the basis of faith, arise? Is this, apart from any real understandings in most faiths, the hounding of one's mind to provide for that interim between life and death. Much of the denial that there is something after our last breath is taken in an attempt to avoid the issue altogether. It was said that after the nine-eleven attacks, where thousands of American were killed, that the churches and synagogs were filled with people not just to pray for the dead and those left behind but by those who thought that this could be just the beginning of the attacks and they were having to think about their own fate, their eternal fate.

In most American hospitals, chaplains walk the corridors daily to bring the message of salvation to all not knowing who would pass away before the next day's visitation. It is at such times that the span between life and death may become critical to one adopting belief and faith in One able to provide salvation from a dark eternity. For others the last moment of repentance comes all too quickly. Orthodox Christianity makes the claim that the diversionary tactics that often succeed in avoidance of soteriological issues is the work of a tempter, deceiver and evil creature variously called, among others, the devil or Satan. In other religions he is absent from religious experience or goes by some other name or other identifying behavior that labels him as evil personified. Witches, or those thought to be witches, have been burned in order to remove the evil indwelling. The superstitious belief held that by killing a human-like personification that the community would avoid the evil that might stand between men, women and God.

Christianity brings the life and death continuum together in the message that Jesus spoke that we were to be fishers of men just as our job may even be to fish. The living of our faith becomes and integral part of the believer's life preaching faith in Christ and the spreading of the Good News about Christ and his sacrificial death on the cross for anyones sins who places trust in Christ's ability to save them from their sins in this life and the torment of the next. All that put their faith, as a result of being caught as a fish, that is their lives caught up in His life, will reign with Jesus in heaven in joy and glory for eternity.

The puzzlement that arises is to not accept this invitation which is totally free. Unlike other religions there is nothing that you can do to gain salvation. Except for holding on to all those earthly desires that tempt us to be atheists or agnostics, their is nothing that prevents man from accepting this free gift. Yes, the enigmatic refusal to follow Christ is a combination of the deceiver's and our own desire to be the god of our own lives even to the probability that we may not return to the soil in finality but enter into an eternity of torment apart from Christ and his free offer of grace to us while we live. This would be holding to the fatal and tempting words that the deceiver gave to mankind in the garden: "you will be gods."

We may be predisposed to consider life after death or a naturalistic physical ending to life in any form, but the alternative to being made righteous by faith in Christ has eternal consequences that the mathematician Pascal would not be willing to gamble. A gamble which must be committed to before falling off the twig.

Chapter 5

The Value and the Meaning
of Life in Death

What is the value of a relatively short life on earth compared to an eternity in Paradise? Certainly Pascal made this point, but to reemphasize, even one hundred years of life is nothing compared to an infinite amount of time, time unending. So to forfeit all of eternity for the few years most of which is often limited by school and work early on and infirmity later on, is not reasonable, based on the wager that Pascal proposed. People avoid this challenge to believe in Christ because, if he is God incarnate, then they are not. He has sovereign control of our lives and not us. For many being one's own god, is too much to give up. We would have to consider someone else in planning our lives. Christianity promises the joining of our soul with a perfected body which is better than a few years of us calling all the shots and being our own god, and a finite god at best, and suffering from an eternity of torment away from God.

The Bible harshly describes the abrupt certainty of death followed by the very next event: we are immediately to be judged. What defense, with out a defensible brief, could a defense possibly be put forth to justify our time on earth? That one may have been a valued member of a firm or corporation has little to argue for you. Maybe the firm itself defended know villains or your corporation contributed to those who polluted neighborhoods in which children were taken ill and died. How could this help you? No one but God's Son, Jesus, led a good sinless life. But even if you had lived an exemplary life and done only good, why would God accept this as a reason to let you into his kingdom? After all if you did not honor God with your life, why would he be inclined to pardon you for your sin of self, the sins that he bore on the cross for sinner's offenses against him ranged from selfishness to genocide.

On the other hand what would allow you to defend yourself against an angry God, who views your sin-guilt not by your defense of villains or a polluting corporation but on the basis of you not putting your trust in him during your life, not placing your faith in his son Jesus Christ but rather trusting in your own understanding. What knowledge could you have that would supersede that of the God who made and sustains the earth.

There are no deals, no payoffs, only you standing before God at the moment of death having rejected his Son who died on a cross for your sins, the sins that you could not avoid for the nature with which you were born into this life, a sinful nature, but with no desire for redemption. Only by the sin-cleansing blood of Jesus Christ can you avoid the verdict of guilty in God's court, and that cleansing comes without cost by placing your faith in Jesus Christ and thereby to give him your life.

And anyway, what sort of value do you propose that will cause God to pardon you from separation from him for eternity? If God is sovereign in this world and the next, why does he need you to have justification of your own values. He is the supreme owner of this world and the next, while you are merely a functionary in this world, this world that one day he will destroy to rebuild a heaven and earth where his will will be carried out flawlessly for his own glory.

Many people believe that they will be able to argue their cases on the basis of their earthly goodness. A perfect God does not tolerate imperfection. The good things you have done do not constitute perfection. But faith in God through his son Jesus Christ can change that fallen nature with which you were born to imperfection to one of righteousness which will be acceptable to God the Father and will ultimately result in your perfection in his heavenly kingdom when you die from this world. This is a gift that God offers through his Son, to be forgiven for the sins you could not avoid by Jesus' death on a cross the perfect and sinless sacrifice for your sin.

Chapter 6

Judging Life Until Death

Most people find life alluring and hold on to every moment especially as they approach the end of their time on earth. Many accept the good values of life as meaningful as evidenced by the unquestioning duty by which they live it, for its routine and reward. Finding the responsibilities worthy of everyday and the rewards brought to bear on a lusty attention to the positive accomplishments pursued, mankind goes on day after day accepting both this good and the inevitable bad. Those that take their own lives believing that the bad outweighs the good may choose to end their life judging it overall a deficit bargain to continue living. The fact that this may not always have been the case does not seem to introduce optimism into the consideration. Anyone's response to the bad, or for that matter the good, seems to depend on the person more than the preponderance of situations or actions deemed good or bad. Such judgmental deficiencies may be responsible for the lethal assessments that bring judgment in death.

But even those that find life good in the main do not often give consideration to the time when life will end for them. What will transpire upon one taking his or her last breathe? Will one ultimately become the atoms and molecules in some other life form? Will the resources or decay merely provide the food for animal life or remain in the ground inanimate?

41

A friend told me that any choice for which afterlife might depend was not something that she could believe. The consequences of this statement did not seem to have the least impact on her demeanor. She acknowledged her bias as if death and its consequences were relatively unimportant. The problem here is that she is not making a decision about death as much as she is deferring judgment about the rest of her life and its conclusion to her agnosticism, her lack of belief.

You can send care packages to the Iraqis and feel better about yourself, but this may have little to nothing to do with any judgment against you being lifted in case their is a reckoning after death. This only makes you feel that you are a good person, at least for a time. Is it easy to assume that not being one of the most wanted by the authorities is good enough for any possible call after death by eternal authority. The care packages were sent without any clear reason why such generosity in helping others has a direct effect on what comes after life on earth. One thing we do know about death is that if it is anything it is not like this life. When people die their remains are returned to the soil or to ashes. Any consideration of what that possible life after death might be has to have benefit of reason, what could decide our fate in a next life. For this is not exclusively a matter of death as it is what we should do now to judge our lives leading up to death and ensuring salvation after death.

The common illusion perpetrated by film and story is that life after death is phantasmic: that the dead float around in this world, their souls released from the material body remain for most eyes and ears just out of reach. Stories from those who have had outer body experiences suggest that they merely floated around unseen looking at themselves and others or some bright light at the end of a tunnel. Judging our lives to end in a sort of diaphanous hovering does not calm any concern that we might be able to dredge up about the possibility of life following one's demise. In fact, if we have no idea about the value of our lives in this life, certainly we have no clear idea about what a life after death must be like. First things first: who are we what are we trying to accomplish on earth and what could an existence beyond this earth require from us after we are gone?

There is the unavoidable fact of death and decay. We have an indisputable fact, what will we do about it? Will we attend to every moment of our lives with plans that are put in place to ward off any disaster except death? Is this loss of life the most important consideration of our lives? Without the right planning we may break our arm, see our house burn down or lose all of our money in the market, but we can recover from all of these mishaps, but not in our earthly form will we recover from death. The real question is what will become of what we think of our selves: body, soul and spirit.

Chapter 7

Spirit, Soul and Body

The integrity of the human being has been addressed since at least the time of the ancient Greeks. Historically when the body died there was inclination to believe that there was something that survived death. Perhaps it was just one's inimitable reputation or possibly an immaterial emergence that carried with it the honor and courage of the deceased but also possibly the essence of that lost life: its memorable moments and its persona. There was also the belief that the emergent quality lost at death was little more than a neutral possession of the life lost in that it left without purpose as the body died. The nebulous metaphysical concerns of life seem to have as much importance to our purpose in life as those easily identifiable milestones in our reasoned progress. Love, caring and beliefs hold us to a meaningful metaphysical purpose just as much as those tangibles of house, car and IRA do. The very concept of living over after death suggests, however, that their was something that this quality lost at death that had some immortal importance that represented the dead and carried something of the dead with it. What is the fate of those intangibles that give our lives and others a sense of value?

We have tended to de-emphasize the realities of death. The loss of the form that death takes in regard to our loved ones. Today we are more likely to close the casket or have a memorial service failing to give the face to face encounter with the end of life. We do not want to look on the cold reality of death. In addition the emphasis on youth at all ages is a withdrawal into Plato's cave in which we choose to look at diversionary reflections perhaps in memory and not at the reality of physical death itself in the cold light of day. We script the reflections that we want to see. We may plan in every other way for death but we do not unexpectedly speak of it, but rather focus unswervingly on stolid attention, on the delusional indefinite and halcyon hold on a tenuous future.

But the spirit and the soul leave the body not just breath and heart beat. The spirit, that vital force that divulges the identifying character of the once living is lost to time. The soul which is believed by most cultures to survive the body and reanimate in a resurrected body, a belief in Christianity, or to remain unencumbered as a shade without substantial moorings floating usually unseen around us, is the final possibilities of those supporting an extended existence.

The soul is not in the purview of science. Belief in an afterlife is a matter of faith. No mortal who has truly left the body, at least there is not proof of such, has ever returned. Despite the fact that this might support a purely physical existence which is lost in its entirety at death of the body, yet the idea of a superseding soul does not seem to be shakeable in those that believe in an afterlife. There seems to be little to infer that a soul is only a surviving entity when the person has warranted a "good" life evaluation like Mother Teresa and not a "bad" one, say, like Hitler. So for those that make this distinction their must be at least two destinations: one often called heaven or paradise and the other hades, hell or even Sheol. The possible separate compartmentalization for the good and for the bad seems invariably to emerge. Where is the distinction between good and bad? How bad does one have to be to enter Hell; how good does one have to be to enter Paradise? Where is the cutoff? The very suggestion that we are guessing at our fate after death and are unable to control the fate of our soul after we die, if we believe we have a soul, makes our existence almost unfair. Being relegated to the fate of the bad may seem unfair, bad luck or to the fate of the good fortuitous.

So what could we do to insure that we would go to a good home for the soul and not a bad one? If we are going to one or the other, how is the decision made and on what basis is that decision based, or is it just a big gamble with no destination being determinate on something done or not done in this life?

The Enlightenment Project did a great disservice to anyone who wanted to find an answer to these questions. Although a softer understanding of the Enlightenment allowed for a religious view of non-scientific considerations, despite the fact that supernatural understandings were mostly rejected, a more stern view disallowed any reasoning not based on the affirmation of the scientific methodology. The only way for reasoning to be found acceptable would be by trusting the mind of man and his ability to test hypotheses based on rational thought. This did not mean that religious considerations could be addressed by logic and reasoned thought. Issues of the soul and death were to be seen as superstitious, and when the body died it rotted and had no soul. This scientific understanding is described as scientistic, but better as scientism, which vehemently and adamantly denies that a soul exists and therefore does not hold to a life after the death of the body. Scientism is the only mode of addressing any issue, since it is the only way to evaluate considerations of life. This approach would breakdown quickly if the metaphysics of a scientist's love for his wife were to be turned only into the chemistry of pheromones and the suitability of his love to merely bear children: strong body and a wide pelvis.

All understanding is only accessible through reason and without man's reasoning nothing can be known. The arrogance of the Enlightenment was that it gave no room for understanding anything without a scientistic spin despite the fact that love, compassion and beauty are not comfortably considered by reason but rather by the heart. The message of the Enlightenment is that these metaphysical ideas, like love and hate, are merely mechanical and physical manifestations of reasoned phenomena. Behaviorists have treated these emotions as purely physical emanations that can be controlled by changing the way the subject is orientated in the physical world around him or her.

Despite the small minded-ness of the Enlightenment argument about death and the soul, the real possibilities is that there may be a soul and death may not be the end of existence. Considering that something may be outside the purview of science and reason, what if there is life after death? Should not Pascal's dare be entertained in consideration that probability and chance might favor a broader consideration of life extension by the soul, as a form of hedging one's bets? Again, death is certain, what occurs at that moment may not be only the first step to the returning of the body to the dust, and, if not, then what are the other possibilities, not what you would wish, which is the mark of a true gambler, but what could be the result of a life extension for which no provision was made. On the positive side it is encouraging to think that the possibilities could include your personality and the deeper elements from your earthly existence that favor love and caring. On the negative side the long shot may be that death leads to nothing at all.

Probably most people through out the world believe that the soul survives the body. Is this a massive hopefulness without any weight of scientific proof, yes, probably? But is it enough to doubt that the belief so widely held is to be ignored with the weight of public opinion being so strong and the looming possibility that the soul does exist and it does live on after the death of the body?

The next consideration based on this belief in a surviving soul would be what is the dispensation of a soul: where will it reside after the body dies? From the ancients we have both good and bad destinations, soul residences which would be idyllic and others where all would find new life in less than a perfect state, but would the body and the soul be reunited to inhabit a new existence whether for good or for bad? Would souls merely waft their way about and find company among other etherial presences? The soul would under these conditions seem wanting a physical presence. To

49

be united with a body would provide the perfect fit for the soul, its original or previous fit. In fact, if a soul were to be reunited with a body like the one it enjoyed in earthly life, then the reincarnation would be fit as both the soul and the body would share commonalities. The body would necessarily be much different because the requirements for a different world, to inhabit a new existence and its environment.

But to reunite the soul, a body and spirit would be the ultimate effect or reincarnation. The spirit-soul is the individual identification of the person. So it would be only right that the new existence would be identifiable by the character and emotions that a life had in developmental experience in an earthly existence. This holism would justify the learning of living the earthly life without having to start living all over possibly without the benefit of the protection of childhood. Reincarnation cannot guarantee this post-existence tapping of human resources for life could be restored in any living form. But could life be known of the earthly existence and could one be ready to join this knowledge and wisdom or experienced failure with the new and complete life.

Chapter 8

The Leavings of Death

If there is nothing after death but the slow deterioration of the body into elemental forms and the progressive deterioration of memories by those that live after you, then life's short duration and value may need to be questioned. If the end of this life terminates our learning, caring and functioning, then what is the big concern for life? We grow and put those things in our life that we see as good only to have them end when the coffin top is closed. This seems to make less sense than there actually being a continuation of life in a different form, an extension of life.

Consider all the relationships that have been left behind upon death. Are you to never continue those developmental interchanges among any of your friends and family? If so, what a loss. Loved ones and patterns of life: work, the things that gave structure to our lives, our interests, our loved ones, these are the scaffolding on which we hang the pieces of our lives and gives us context for living.

One's thought may turn to those daily staples to which we will no longer experience. The sun and shadows of our familiar surroundings, the gentle breezes that move the leaves and bring them to the ground in fall and our pets that will play in the yard without someone to throw the tennis ball for them.

These are some of the constants when we no longer so remain.

The constancy of our workplace upon our death will be just a hiccup in the operation of things. One day to attend the funeral and after that the same old schedule as if we were never there. Someone sitting at our desk or operating the machines and instruments that we once looked on not only as ours but of us in a more emotional sense.

It would seem that life would be less than meaningless, a horrible joke, if we only stirred for a while and then lost all in the physical realm taking with it the loss of the spirit and the soul. It may seem that leaving a legacy of descendants and worldly effects that will continue to circulate ones name after death is not much of a consolation for a life, possibly a hard life, of learning and doing. If death is the end, were the ideas and offspring we left worth the weight of worry, pain and disappointments that we suffered for so many years?

At best we will be left in memory for something if our contributions are searched out. History has given us the compounded interests of the architects of time. Each contribution giving us a lighter load during our lives, making life easier and adding to our understanding of ourselves and the world in which we live. Each of us is an accumulation of those discoveries and ideas that have made us healthier on the whole and happier when appropriately experienced.

Death should never take the life that we have lived from us. It has been said that the reason there must be something after death is that we have lived a life of experience and knowledge and for all of that for the good to go to the grave is unimaginable. The loss of who we are is indeed a great loss. This must be addressed as a reason for there being life after death.

What is left behind will not necessarily be credited to us personally. The buildings that have been built depended on the architect and workers. Each bridge spans the lives of many who have given their work and possibly their lives to enshrine their contribution in steal against time and weather. Part of the enjoyment of our lives has been a gift left behind for us to build on and for others that follow after us. Collectively with the help of generations we are to be made better for our efforts. Material, worldly contributions to our comfort and the ideas that are given not to be taken back from our knowledge are passed along to those who may give continuity to our lives and hope for the future.

No one leaves this earth without having left an imprint on the planet. We are to live on in the understanding of what it is to be human and what can and has been done to allow humanity to spread among people of all time, if not exclusively in deed, then in the knowledge of what we were and what we passed along.

Pascal offers a hope for new existence in death. Christ rose from the grave, offers eternal life with Him and the Father and the Holy Spirit which will end well with us in this life when we place our faith in life and in death with the Father through our faith in his Son. Death will separate us for all we know on this earth, but Christ can give us new life, perfected in Him and an eternity in Paradise.

Chapter 9

The Takings of Life

Life will be lost, for this is a certainty. Memories of the dead will be lost by those that live on. We the living lose the image and the voice and the smiles that once entrained our vision of loved ones. Life however may be lost while one is still alive. If our health is slipping away, the worry or fear of dying my take away our lives before we leave this earth. Perhaps life may seem not worth living if our wealth is lost. If we have to deal daily with waning health issues our lives are not lived to the fullest even as we plan our days in order to ward off the worst pain or incapacity. When we have to give every consideration of our life, how we will be able to afford living with any degree of grace, our life is being taken from us. The life that we would have accepted and never considered our ultimate fate.

When we are given to the necessity of juggling doctors appointments and health regimens for our survival we are closing off an important time of insight by the very events and time spent marking our surrender to indigency or infirmity, or we disregard the signs of age and decreased health and push on as if we were never going to die. Total dedication of our last years is failed in our unreal grasp at life without a sensible respect for the ultimate reality of our demise.

A predilection for health and our management of our physical and financial needs often prevent us from giving others a chance to help us deal with the reality of death. Attending to ones immediate needs during this time, when we are coming close to the end of our life, becomes a diversion from the concern that should be at the forefront of ours and our caretakers and loved one's thoughts. If the legal prospects of our imminent death are crowding out the thoughts of the reality of life's finality, that is death's power, then we have given the wrong emphasis to our preparation for death. We hear regrets like he or she did not get to see her grands grow up, or at least he or she is not suffering any more. How do you know that? You don't. It just makes everyone feel better about their own lack of consideration of death.

There is no doubt that death can be acute in the way we are mowed down with little pretense or warning, but death is also at times unexpressive or at least incremental in its taking. We do not see that by the hour or the day times, the number of days that we have on earth, for it is an incremental deduction from our total number of days. As we are reminded: we live only four score and seventy years, or Emerson says: "nature cannot be cheated: man's life is but seventy salads long." What we know is that we die incrementally and often without registering the loss of the life that is being taken from us. Some see little of those salad days; some are granted many more green salads than can be explained. But it could be said that we lose our lives everyday. Then why do we not consider what we are loosing by day, month or year? If we are even given a chance to register the lose in effect, the years may seem to flow by us like a river, and as Heraclitus reminds us: we can never step into that same river twice. The time, the environment is constantly being replaced where we think we stand firmly in time. It looks just like the water from an hour or a month or a year, but the environment has changed as new water is seen, as old water flows from us.

The water looks the same: the same job, the same co-workers and the same business perhaps, but you and I are moving inextricably to our deaths although it may appear without close scrutiny that all is the same. Often the mirror can monitor the change in one's face, but some age more gracefully and do not note the change in wrinkles and the bags under the eyes.

In the book by Leo Tolstoy, *The Death of Ivan Illyich,* the events leading up to the death of Ivan Illyich are chronicled. Ivan does not die well. He has misgivings about almost everything, his wife, his life after the pronouncement of disease all of which preempts dying by his loathing of his last days and the torment of the spirit in perpetual pain. This is the dying of the spirit, preliminary to joining the so called choir eternal. He died for a long time before the actual event which took his last breath. Death takes life from all of us eventually, but when all one has to do in the meantime is posit regrets for one's life, then death takes more than our lives it takes our liveliness and the important time for memories. Instead of looking back on the good life that we have had, the good fortune to live, we find, as Ivan Illyich did, that concentrating on the negatives of life take the good times and good experiences: it robs us of the best we had and had to offer.

Death should never take the life that we have lived from us. It has been said before: the reason there must be something after death is that we have lived a life of experience and knowledge, so hard and for all of that to go to the grave is unimaginable. The loss of who we are is indeed a great loss.

And what if we do not live again? We will leave the structure of time and place as we only prepared the soil in the past and now someone else is furrowing the ground for the replanting. Another harvest and harvest will render the garden as we fade in the memory of fellow workers and management. We will become unremembered with time, but even if we were to be remembered it would be for specific reasons interrogating specific facts while one's identity may lost in that remembrance. All of your personal impact on lives will be lost, lost in time. We will leave the structure of time and place. We will become un-remembered with time, ; as in Ridley Scott's *Blade Runner* movie, Rutger Hauer gives us the "death" speech in which he says that all memories will be lost as tears in the rain.

Chapter 9

God and Death

The expression that "there are no atheists in a fox hole," points out that most people who are avid, so called, God botherers, in the near close of their lives, may find a need to at least consider God. This may never happen with the resolve of the dyed in the wool atheists and those who lose their lives unexpectedly, say, as the result of a fatal car accident or an unexpected fatal heart attack, but most will give at least a nod to the possibility that they may be able to do something in their remaining time to justify their case for God smiling on their lives. If they so muster effective belief presupposing the existence of a God as well as an afterlife in heaven or hell, then there is the hope of taking the dare to attain eternal life. More importantly of concern is that if there is a God he is not a capricious godlike creatures that plays with men as if they were toys, but a serious and resolute God.

We are inclined to consider the existence or divinity when distinguishing between lives that are good and evil. In the past evil has been treaded on lightly as an over dramatization of undesirable acts, but, in regard to recent terror attack, the word has resurfaced and has found new devotees in broader circles. But if there are good and evil acts and people who do them, then how could one consider their rewards or penalties, respectively?

Many of the evil ones and their acts will never be judged and sentenced in this life. This has been responsible for proposing the possibility that judgment comes for those after death. Justice, if we commit to it, must come sometime to have a weight of evenness and fairness, further suggesting that perhaps justice may be served after death. To imagine that evil may never be judged must make us imagine that this life is dangerous, fraught with peril thus compromising any view that this life and our still beautiful world is somehow tainted and unworthy of our favorable attention. To deny evil its judgment, in life or in death, can only bring a sense of pessimism to our daily lives and the pallor of the egregious incapacity of this world.

What if, on the other hand their were a God and he would ultimately judge evil after we have left this earth, after evil had escaped detection and punishment perhaps in this life. This not only would change our view of evil pervading our view of life but would satisfy our need for evil to be judged and punished, if not here, then after death in a completely new existence which would not permit escape from punishment.

But God may find good, if he does exist, yet he is perfect and sets the highest bar for goodness unattainable for his earthlings. So the evils and the evil ones might be judged, but what would allow the non-evil, which we do not like to think of ourselves, from escaping the wrath of a perfect God. Would a perfect God, unlike that of the Roman and Greek gods, accept us willingly into their presence? These were not always gracious to man, and they certainly were not perfect and void of all mean motives. To find our way into the presence of a perfect God, we must be perfect, for although we may not be evil in the common sense of the term we are not perfect and would not be acceptable to a perfect God. We would not be good enough for his perfection.

This is where the God of Christianity makes a strong argument for man finding acceptance for imperfect man. He has solved the problem of not only evil itself but of our less than perfect lives which must be lumped in with evil as sin. For us to be in his eternal kingdom to be with a perfect God we may be given the righteous of God that will change our sinful nature and ultimately take away our sin.

God through Christ has made a way for us with imperfect morals to be made perfect before him. Christ, God's son, is perfect. He came and gave himself to die for sin, which we all have in our nature as imperfections, whether we are evil by earth's standards or just mostly good. A sinless God took our sin on himself and died on a cross - a perfect man paying our sin debt for sinful mankind - and for those of us who accept the gift of eternal life based on our faith in Christ we are cleansed and made to be seen as perfect before God the Father. We may enter into God's kingdom and spend eternity with Him free of sin and guilt and ultimately made perfect like Him. The alternative is to hope we make it to a new existence as good people. This is little more than trying to qualify by testing without having meaningful knowledge of the examination. Those that believe that God has disposed of our examination, if we put our life and our death in his hands by faith with only the acknowledgement that we need him to take away our sins and to lead us in this life and the next are those to whom Pascal was speaking.

How do we gain this faith? By giving our lives through our admission of sin and then by unfaltering trust in Christ as our savior and God who will not only deliver us into his Kingdom at death but will guide and direct us in this life growing in righteousness as we are made righteous through obedience to him and thereby made acceptable to God the Father. Without this we dare to chance eternal death in torment.

Conclusion

If you are afraid to die, you must have little reason to believe that death is not the end of existence. If you are not afraid then you must have reason to believe that there has been provision made for you after death, or you do not believe their is anything after death but decay. To not believe or indeed to believe in life after death and to not fear, may be irrational. Without life after death means the body will cease to be and all knowledge, wisdom, personality and memories will also be lost. Those that do not think they know about life after death but never considered it are truly lost. A short eight or nine decades for the long-lived, does not challenge the potential of an eternity after death. The span of eternity which we have no reason to doubt stands as a challenge to reason. Those that believe that the world is billions of years old would be hard pressed to find the remaining time on earth as short or short in some other physical existence in another place. Life has gone on before us why not long after us. Furthermore, not to have a plan for how you might fare after death is also of concern. Did you do enough good, or did you do too many bad or evil acts that a possible good afterlife may be in doubt? Does God determine our future afterlife as the Egyptians had imagined? The heart of the dead was weighed against a feather to determine whether you lived a good and worthy life or you lived a bad or evil life and would have an afterlife of punishment and suffering. By our nature we tend to do wrong even when we sometimes do not realize it, and this may be in part the purpose of juries and courtrooms to settle the difficult misbehaviors of morals. All of us are imperfect - the only nature that God can accept is perfection. By this standard, the toughest of all measures, we are lost.

Not to think about death before you die is counter intuitive for one who has possibly planned for every contingency in life from the cradle to the grave. A single leap of faith by which you commit to God's plan for making you acceptable to live with him in eternity has, as we have explored in previous chapters, explained how justice escaped here on earth can be made right, how our past experience and knowledge is not to be waisted because of an afterlife and Christianity provides a way of understanding how evil, that we all have committed can be offset by the gift of Christ's death on the cross to take away not our sin alone but, as we commit to Christ in faith, also the very sin nature with which we were born and which made us unable to escape evil and sin. God's grace to those that accept his Lordship will also in effect glorify God the Father. God is worthy of being gloried by his children who are faithful to his name by living lives that honor God and trust in Christ as his children, to love and obey his Word, the Bible.

Dickens visited death in the familiar story, *The Christmas Carol*. Scrooge survived his business partner Marley by seven years to the night that his partner's ghost came to warn him of his deeds and to tell of the visitation by three spirits: past, present and future spirits. Scrooge was frozen with fear. He had seen the face of Marley in the door that very night and begun to think about him. His partner's name was still on the door of their business, but when he came home after work he was scared and went through the rooms to check for anything or anyone who might be in the house in which he alone dwelled. Scrooge seemed to be turned by his spirit visitors little by little, from the spirit Past he saw his failures as a man, by the spirit present he was to see the Scrooge of today and the hard man he had grown into and by the ghost of the future he was confronted with the reality of death.

Scrooge, from this lesson in time and folly, became a different man. His look at the future showed him his own tombstone, his name cut deep into the alabaster. his face to face with death is not the normal way that the reality of death is faced. By no warning, the warning of impending demise, but we do not get to see our death; we do not preview it for our reclamation, if that is necessary; we are not weaned. Not in the loss of our life but in the living of that life. We know that it will happen and when it does it is final and their is at that time and here after not again will we be able to change our lives. To misquote Dylan Thomas, do not go gently into that dark night, without knowing your destination. Give your life to God though faith in Christ now. Take responsibility for your life and your death and God will honor you through eternity and adopt you into his holy family. In John 3:16, we are told that God loved the world so much that all that place their faith in Jesus Christ, God's Son, will have everlasting life with Him. Take Pascal's dare.